W9-BWU-560

Date: 2/15/12

J 552 RAU
Rau, Dana Meachen,
Rocks and minerals /

PALM BEACH COUNTY
LIBRARY SYSTEM
3650 SUMMIT BLVD.
WEST PALM BEACH, FL 33406

21st Century Skills Library

REAL WORLD SCIENCE

ROCKS AND MINERALS

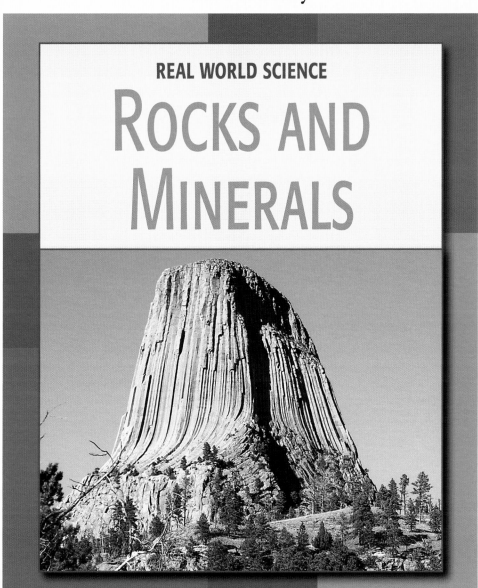

Dana Meachen Rau

Cherry Lake Publishing
Ann Arbor, Michigan

Published in the United States of America by Cherry Lake Publishing
Ann Arbor, Michigan
www.cherrylakepublishing.com

Content Adviser: Laura Graceffa, middle school science teacher; BA degree in science, Vassar College; MA degrees in science and education, Brown University

Photo Credits: Cover and page 1, © poutnik/Shutterstock; page 4, © koer/Shutterstock; page 6, Photo Researchers, Inc.; page 7, © Gontar/Shutterstock; page 9, Javier Trueba/Photo Researchers, Inc.; page 11, © Jaci Harmsen/Shutterstock; page 13, © Steve Estvanik/Shutterstock; page 15, Photo Researchers, Inc.; page 17, © Four Oaks/Shutterstock; page 18, Maury Aaseng; page 21, © Shutterstock; page 23, © Christopher Edwin Nuzzaco/Shutterstock; page 25, © Keith Tarrier/Shutterstock; page 27, © Philip Lange/Shutterstock

Copyright ©2009 by Cherry Lake Publishing
All rights reserved. No part of this book may be reproduced or utilized in any form or by any means without written permission from the publisher.

Library of Congress Cataloging-in-Publication Data

Rau, Dana Meachen, 1971-
Rocks and minerals / Dana Meachen Rau.
  p. cm.—(Real world science)
Includes index.
ISBN-13: 978-1-60279-463-4
ISBN-10: 1-60279-463-4
1. Rocks—Juvenile literature. 2. Rock-forming minerals—Juvenile literature. I. Title. II. Series.

QE432.2.R28 2009
552—dc22   2008049663

Cherry Lake Publishing would like to acknowledge the work of
The Partnership for 21st Century Skills.
Please visit www.21stcenturyskills.org *for more information.*

TABLE OF CONTENTS

CHAPTER ONE

IT'S ELEMENTARY! MAKING UP MINERALS

The world is filled with rocks and minerals of many different shapes, sizes, and colors.

Time to bake a cake! A recipe will tell you what ingredients to use.

Most cakes have flour, sugar, and eggs. If you add apples you'll have

one kind of cake. If you add peanut butter you'll have another. The

rocks and minerals that make up the Earth's surface, or **crust**, are like

that, too. Rocks and minerals have certain "ingredients." The mix of ingredients makes each type of rock and mineral unique.

What is a mineral? Minerals are the ingredients in rocks. They are found in nature, but they are not living things. Minerals are made up of basic substances called **elements**. There are just over 100 elements on Earth. The most common elements in minerals are oxygen and silicon. These two plus six others form most minerals.

There are more than 3,500 known minerals. Some minerals contain just

Below are some of the properties scientists use to identify minerals.

Color: Some minerals are always the same color while others come in a variety of colors.

Streak: You can rub a mineral on a piece of tile to see the color of a mineral's powder. The streak color is not always the same color as the mineral itself.

Luster: Scientists use words such as dull, greasy, pearly, and metallic to describe the way light bounces off a mineral.

Cleavage and **Fracture:** Cleavage describes when a mineral breaks with smooth, flat surfaces. Fracture describes when a mineral breaks with uneven surfaces.

Hardness: The Mohs Scale is a chart that helps determine the hardness of a mineral. Hardness is tested by scratching a sample with certain tools or with other minerals.

Transparency: Light passes through some minerals but not others.

Crystal Shape: Certain shapes help identify mineral type.

Galena is a common mineral that breaks into cubes when it splits.

one type of element. For instance, the metals gold and silver are both

minerals. Both contain just one element. Most minerals are a combination

of elements. Minerals that contain silicon and oxygen are called silicates.

Quartz is a silicate. It is one of the most common minerals on Earth.

With so many kinds of elements, how do scientists tell them apart?

Think about some of the differences between you and a friend. Do you

have different eye colors? Is one of you taller? Does one of you have longer

hair? These and other features are what make you…you. Minerals also

have certain features, or **properties**. Scientists look at the properties of

minerals to tell them apart.

Quartz is easy to identify by the shape of its crystals.

One mineral property is **cleavage**. Cleavage is the way a mineral splits into pieces. For instance, mica splits into thin sheets. Galena breaks into cubes.

Minerals also differ in **luster**. Luster is how light bounces off a mineral. The mineral pyrite is shiny. The mineral celadonite is dull. Some minerals, like beryl, are even transparent. You can see right through them.

Color is another property of minerals. Turquoise is blue and zorite is pink. But topaz can be blue, yellow, brown, or red.

Another important property is a mineral's hardness. Hardness is a test to see how easily a mineral is scratched. Talc is the softest because all of the other minerals can scratch it. Diamond is the hardest because no other known mineral can scratch it.

Scientists can also look at the type of **crystals** a mineral forms. Sometimes in nature, minerals are not solid. They might be **dissolved**

The largest crystals in the world are found in the Cave of Crystals in Chihuahua, Mexico.

in the water of a stream, or in water underground. Water then **evaporates**, or escapes into the air. The mineral stays behind and forms crystals.

Some crystals are tiny. Others are huge. Their size depends on how much room they have to expand. The largest natural crystals ever found are in Chihuahua, Mexico. They are gypsum crystals more than 20 feet (6 m) long.

Crystals form in different shapes. Some crystals are cubes. Others have six sides. Crystals might grow like branches or bumps. Quartz crystals have flat sides. Asbestos crystals grow in strands.

REAL WORLD SCIENCE CHALLENGE

To learn how crystals form, ask an adult to help you boil water. Pour about ½ cup (118 ml) of the boiling water into a glass measuring cup. Add a spoonful of table salt and stir. The salt will dissolve in the water. Keep adding more salt and stirring until the salt no longer dissolves. Pour the salt water into a pie plate until you've covered the bottom of the plate. Then place the pie plate in the sun. After about six hours, check your pie plate. What do you see?

(Turn to page 29 for the answer)

Scientists can look at the shape a crystal forms. This property, along with cleavage, luster, hardness, color, and many more, help them decide the type of mineral sample they have.

CHAPTER TWO

ROCKIN' RECIPES! ROCKS AND HOW THEY FORM

The faces of four presidents are carved into the igneous rock of Mount Rushmore.

Elements are the ingredients of minerals. Minerals are the ingredients of

rocks. Rocks take thousands and even millions of years to form. Rocks are

made of different mixtures of minerals. They don't all look the same. Rocks can

be smooth or rough. They can be all one color or filled with flecks or stripes.

Learning & Innovation Skills

Aliens have landed! These are not little green men, but alien rocks called meteorites. Chunks of rocks and metal travel through the solar system. Sometimes one gets so close to Earth it falls through the atmosphere. When it crashes to the ground, it makes a hole called a crater. The Barringer Meteorite Crater is in the Arizona desert. It was the first crater identified as being made by a meteorite. The hole in the sandstone formed almost 50,000 years ago. It is almost a mile (1.6 km) wide. More than 100 other meteorite craters have been found. Scientists study craters to learn about the history of our planet and these "visitors" from space.

There are three basic types of rock. The most common is **igneous** rock. Earth's crust is made up mostly of igneous rock. Two of the most common types of igneous rock are granite and basalt.

Like many types of igneous rock, granite forms underground. Deep below Earth's crust is a layer of rock so hot that it is a liquid. This liquid rock is called **magma**. Sometimes magma gets trapped in pockets of solid rock. It cools over thousands of years. Because it cools slowly, the minerals form large crystals. You can see crystals of the minerals feldspar, mica, and quartz in a piece of granite.

Other igneous rocks form above ground. Hot magma sometimes comes to the surface through a volcano on

When sediment settles on the bottoms of rivers, lakes, and oceans, it may turn into sedimentary rock.

land or in the sea. Magma that reaches Earth's surface is called **lava**. Rock forms when the lava cools. Lava cools much faster above ground than underground. So crystals don't have as much time to form. This is what happens with basalt. Crystals form in basalt as it cools. But they are much smaller than the ones in granite. Sometimes lava cools so quickly, crystals have no time to form. This is what happens with obsidian, a rock that looks like black glass.

The second type of rock is **sedimentary** rock. It makes up the top layers of Earth's crust. Sediment is solid matter such as sand or gravel that is carried by water or wind. These bits of earth settle on the bottoms of rivers, lakes, and oceans, with layers building up over time. The layers above push on the layers below. This pressure makes the sediment harden into rock.

REAL WORLD SCIENCE CHALLENGE

Sediment is often carried by water, and then left on the bottom of lakes. Layers pile on top of each other and can form into sedimentary rock. But how does sediment settle out of water to the bottom of a lake? To find out, you will need a clear plastic container with a lid. Scoop up about 1/3 cup (78 ml) of dirt or sand from outside. Place it in the container. Then add water to almost fill the container. Put on the lid and shake it up so that the dirt is well mixed with the water. Take off the lid and set it aside. Look at it after 10 minutes. Do you see any changes to the mixture? Look at it again after an hour. Now what does it look like? Leave it out for a few days. How long does it take all the dirt to settle out of the water? How is this like what happens at the bottom of a lake?

(Turn to page 29 for the answer)

Metamorphic rock (pictured) forms with great heat or great pressure underground.

There are many types of sedimentary rock. Sandstone is one type.

It is made from sand. Limestone is another. It is made mostly from the

skeletons of sea creatures.

The third type of rock is **metamorphic** rock. It forms when one type

of rock changes into another type of rock. This can only happen with

heat and pressure. Inside the Earth, hot magma sometimes pushes into

Learning & Innovation Skills

You can look back in time by studying the layers of sedimentary rock. The lowest layers might be millions of years old. Sometimes scientists find **fossils** in sedimentary rock. Fossils are the remains of plants and animals from long ago that have left an impression in rock.

In Rockville, Connecticut, people accidentally discovered fossils of dinosaur tracks. A construction truck unearthed a large slab of rock covered with them. These tracks were made 200 million years ago. Sediment covered the tracks. The land above became rock. The rock became buried deep in the ground until the truck accidentally dug it up! Now you can view these tracks at the site where they were discovered, now called Dinosaur State Park.

the crust. Then it heats the surrounding rocks. The temperature is so hot that the minerals change into new minerals. They make new types of rock.

The pressure underground is also very strong. Some rocks push and squeeze rocks nearby. This also makes minerals change. Marble is a type of metamorphic rock that comes from limestone. Shale is a kind of sedimentary rock. It can turn into the metamorphic rock slate.

A rock you pick up from the ground might be millions of years old. It is a result of the strong forces of nature at work in and on the Earth.

CHAPTER THREE

ON THE MOVE! THE ROCK CYCLE

Stalactites and stalagmites grow in caves as water dissolves minerals in limestone.

Rocks are always changing. They break down. They reform. They turn into other rocks. The process of rocks forming into other types of rock is called the rock cycle.

Though you can't feel it, the rocky earth beneath your feet is always moving. The Earth's crust is made up of vast pieces of rock called plates. These plates slowly shift away from or closer to each other. When they spread apart, they make cracks. When they push together, they create folds.

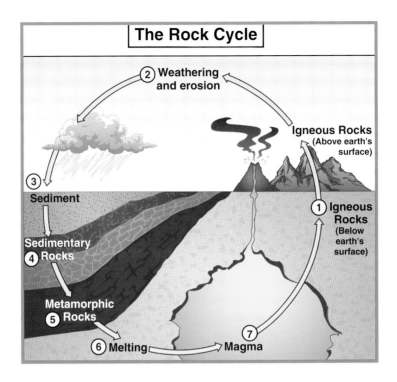

The Rock Cycle

② Weathering and erosion

Igneous Rocks (Above earth's surface)

③

Sediment

④ Sedimentary Rocks

① Igneous Rocks (Below earth's surface)

⑤ Metamorphic Rocks

⑥ Melting

⑦ Magma

These movements can expose deep layers of igneous rock that were once far below the surface. Then this rock is exposed to water and wind.

Water and wind **erode**, or break down, the rock into sediment. This sediment may settle in layers. These layers could become sedimentary rock.

Heat and pressure underground could change the sedimentary rock into metamorphic rock. This metamorphic rock may become magma. The magma may become igneous rock again. That is the

rock cycle.

Wind and water are the powerful forces that erode

rocks. Water in rivers and streams runs over rocks

and smoothes the rough edges. Rain also causes rocks

to change. The White Cliffs of Dover in England have

been eroding for thousands of years. The sea and rain

have been chipping away at these soft chalk cliffs.

Water can also seep into cracks and dissolve minerals

inside the rock. Caves are formed by rainwater carving

out spaces in limestone. Sometimes water dissolves

minerals in the limestone. The minerals may reform

into stalactites and stalagmites. Stalactites are formed

Geodes are rocks that are rough on the outside but have a "secret" on the inside. They are hollow and lined with crystals. No one knows exactly how geodes form. But scientists think that geodes form inside pockets of air trapped in rock. Water may leak into these spaces. Sometimes the water contains dissolved minerals. These minerals form crystals around the edges of the space. The empty space in the center may fill with crystals, too.

from the minerals left behind when water drips from the ceiling of a cave. They look like rock icicles hanging from the ceiling. Stalagmites are formed from the drips that hit the cave floor. They grow taller as more water drips on them.

REAL WORLD SCIENCE CHALLENGE

Ice is just frozen water. But it can be a powerful force in changing rocks.

Fill a clear plastic container about halfway up with water. Mark the water's level on the outside with a permanent marker. Place the container in the freezer. Check back after about 24 hours. Mark the ice level on the outside of the container.

Is the level of the ice the same as the level of the water? How could this affect rocks?

(Turn to page 29 for the answer)

Water inside a crack can also freeze. Water expands when it freezes into ice. The ice pushes on the crack like a wedge and makes pieces break off.

Glaciers also rub against rocks. Glaciers are huge, slow-moving sheets of solid snow and ice. As they move, they carve out deep valleys. You can see the land left behind by glaciers at Glacier Bay National Park in Alaska.

Even plants and animals can make rocks change. The roots of plants sometimes grow into cracks in rocks. As the roots get larger, they can force rocks to break apart. Animals that make burrows for shelter may also affect rocks. Their burrows become pathways for water to travel to rocks once hidden by soil.

Wind also breaks rocks down into sediment. Wind picks up bits of sand and blows them onto other rocks. This wears away the surface of soft rock like sandpaper. Wind erosion sometimes creates odd-shaped rock

Wind eroded these rocks into mushroom shapes in Mexico's Copper Canyon.

formations, such as mushroom rocks. Mushroom rocks tower high. But

they have a thin base. They can be found all over the world, such as in the

in deserts of Egypt and Israel, where blowing sand has worn away the rock.

REAL WORLD SCIENCE CHALLENGE

To see erosion at work, try this simple experiment in your shower. All you need is a new bar of soap, a ruler, and a notebook to record what you observe. Before you begin, measure the bar of soap. Then in your notebook, write the date, the measurements, and a description of your soap. (Does it have square edges or writing on it? Is it all one color, or does it have swirls or stripes?) Use the soap as you shower each day. Every other day for two weeks, wait for your soap to dry, then measure it and describe it in your notebook. How did its shape and appearance change over two weeks? What caused this change?

(Turn to page 29 for the answer)

All of these bits of sediment will eventually form into new rocks.

The rock cycle reuses the same minerals and rocks over and over again.

Scientists believe Earth is 4.5 billion years old. Nature has been using the

same ingredients to make rocks since Earth began.

CHAPTER FOUR

ROCK JOBS! ROCKS AND MINERALS AT WORK

Computer circuit boards need crystals to run.

Did you brush your teeth today? Did you use a computer? Did you go to school? You could not have done any of these things without rocks and minerals. Your toothpaste contains minerals. Your computer needs crystals to run. The sidewalk around your school and the bricks on the walls are made from ground-up rocks.

A geologist is a scientist who studies rocks. You can see what it's like to be a geologist by starting your own rock collection. You'll need a backpack and a magnifying glass, a notebook and pencil, small plastic bags, and a field guide. A field guide is a book listing types of rocks and minerals. You can find one at your local library.

You can search for samples in your own backyard. Or choose a woods, park, or beach nearby. Put each sample in a bag. Keep a description of what it looks like in your notebook. Look in the field guide to try to decide the type of rock you have found. When you get home, clean your samples carefully with warm water, soap, and a toothbrush. Find a place to display them, such as an empty egg carton or a box with dividers. Be sure to label each sample.

People have found uses for rocks and minerals all through time. In the Stone Age, hunters made axes from rocks. When people started farming, they used stones to grind corn. Civilizations grew, and people carved beautiful sculptures out of marble. Today, you use a mineral called graphite when you write with a pencil.

Rock is a strong building material. It is used to make concrete and brick. Buildings dating back thousands of years were made with concrete and brick. You can still see one of these ancient buildings in Rome, Italy. The Colosseum was a stadium where Romans watched gladiator

The Colosseum in Rome was built more than 2,000
years ago from brick, marble, and stone.

fights. The Colosseum's foundation is made of concrete. The rest is

made from brick, marble, and stone. The Colosseum was built more

than 2,000 years ago. These materials are still used in buildings today.

Today, we also use crystals. They are found in many tools we use.

Some of these crystals are grown in a laboratory. Their growth can be

controlled so that they reach certain sizes and shapes. Computers rely

on silicon crystals. Watches use quartz crystals to keep perfect time.

Your home is filled with rocks and minerals. You brush your teeth

each morning with minerals. Toothpaste contains fluorite and calcite.

These minerals clean your teeth and protect them from decay. You can

find other minerals in your bathroom, too. Powder is made from talc.

Sun block contains the mineral zinc.

One way to get needed minerals from the ground is by mining.

Mining is separating a mineral from the rock surrounding it. Mines

snake deep underground. People and machines chip away at the rock

to take out needed minerals.

Metallic ores are metal mineral deposits that are mined.

Iron, aluminum, and copper are metallic ores that can be made

into many products. Forks and spoons are made of steel. Steel is a

combination of iron and other elements. A soda can is made from

An excavator in a stone pit mine uncovers minerals for use in many different products.

aluminum. Pots are sometimes made of copper. A sink faucet is made

of chrome.

People also mine for **gems**. Gems, such as diamonds, rubies, and

emeralds, are very valuable forms of minerals. A gem is a single crystal of

a mineral cut and polished in a certain way. This reveals its bright color,

luster, and transparency. The Cullinan Diamond is one of the largest

diamonds ever mined. It was found in South Africa in the early 1900s.

Learning & Innovation Skills

The Hope Diamond is probably the most famous gem in history. The stone is a deep blue color. It was first found in 1642 in India. Today, it is on display at the Smithsonian Institution in Washington, D.C. It has been owned by many people. It has also been cut again to increase its beauty.

Some people believe the Hope Diamond is cursed. They believe the diamond was stolen from a sacred statue in India. They think that whoever owns the diamond will have bad luck. They blame the diamond for any bad luck that has happened to its owners.

The diamond was cut into separate gems. The largest of these is now the head of the queen of England's royal scepter.

We often say that gems are precious and valuable. But all rocks and minerals are precious and valuable to us on Earth. Nature mixes ingredients to make a wide variety of them. The strong forces deep inside and on the surface of Earth constantly shape and change these rocks and minerals.

REAL WORLD SCIENCE CHALLENGE ANSWERS

Chapter One

Page 10

After about six hours (depending on how dry the day is), the water will be gone. The bottom of the pie plate will be covered with salt crystals. This is like what happens in nature. The ocean is made of saltwater. When seawater evaporates, it leaves salt crystals behind just like in your experiment.

Chapter Two

Page 14

Combining the dirt and water makes a dark, cloudy mixture. After just ten minutes, you'll see some of the dirt settling out of the water to the bottom of the container. After an hour, you'll see even more. After a few days, most of the sediment will be on the bottom. The water will be much clearer. This is like what happens in a lake. The dirt mixed in with water eventually falls to the bottom. Over time, layers of this sediment pile up on top of each other.

Chapter Three

Page 20

The level of the ice will be higher than the level of the water. That is because water expands, or takes up more space, when it is frozen. In nature, water often seeps into cracks in rocks. If temperatures go below freezing, the water will turn to ice. The ice will push on the sides of a crack and break apart the rock.

Page 22

You'll find that over two weeks, your soap has decreased in size. Any rough edges have been worn smooth. The running water of the shower caused this change. It also changed because you rubbed the soap on a washcloth or on your body. This is like what happens to a rock in a running river. The water constantly flows over the rock, making it smoother and smaller. It rubs against other rocks, too. All of these actions wear away the rock.

Glossary

cleavage (KLEE-vij) the way a mineral breaks along flat planes

crust (KRUST) the rocky surface layer of Earth

crystals (KRIS-tulz) geometric shapes formed by minerals

dissolved (di-ZOLVD) mixed (as a solid) into a liquid so that the solid seems to disappear

elements (EL-uh-mentz) substances made up of only one type of atom

erode (ee-ROHD) to wear away rock through natural forces such as water and/or wind

evaporates (ee-VAP-or-aytz) when water or other liquid enters the air as a gas

fossils (FAH-sulz) remains of plants or animals from long ago that are imprinted in rock

gems (JEMZ) single crystals cut and polished in a way to make them shiny and beautiful

igneous (IG-nee-us) a type of rock made from magma or lava

lava (LA-vuh) magma that comes to the Earth's surface

luster (LUS-ter) how light reflects off an object; shininess

magma (MAG-muh) hot liquid rock underground

metallic ores (muh-TAL-ik ORZ) mineral deposits removed from rocks by mining

metamorphic (met-a-MOR-fik) a type of rock made when another type of rock is changed by heat and pressure

properties (PROP-ur-teez) the characteristics of an object

sedimentary (se-di-MEN-tar-ee) a type of rock made from layers of solid matter such as sand and gravel that has been pressed tightly together

FOR MORE INFORMATION

Books

Allaby, Michael. *National Geographic Visual Encyclopedia of Earth*. Washington, DC: National Geographic Children's Books, 2008.

Matthews, Rupert. *Visual Factfinder: Rocks and Fossils*. Essex, England: Miles Kelly, 2008.

Pellant, Chris, and Helen Pellant. *Rock Stars: Crystals and Gemstones*. Pleasantville, NY: Gareth Stevens, 2008.

Symes, R.F. *Eyewitness Books: Rocks and Minerals*. New York: DK Children, 2008.

Web Sites

The Children's Museum of Indianapolis: Geo Mysteries
www.childrensmuseum.org/geomysteries/index2.html
Get answers to questions about rocks and minerals.

Geology for Kids
www.kidsgeo.com/
Learn lots about various geology topics, and play geology games.

Mineralogy Society of America: Mineralogy 4 Kids
www.minsocam.org/MSA/K12/K_12.html
Discover the minerals all around you and how scientists test their properties.

Rock Hounds
www.fi.edu/fellows/fellow1/oct98/index2.html
Gather rocks with tips from this site, then test your knowledge with quizzes and puzzles.

Think Quest Jr.: This Planet Really Rocks!
http://library.thinkquest.org/J002289/
Explore this site, packed with information about rocks and how they form.

INDEX

ABOUT THE AUTHOR

Dana Meachen Rau has written more than 200 books for children in preschool to middle school. Her books span subjects of science, history, geography, biography, hobbies, crafts, and reading. Mrs. Rau loves hiking and rock climbing, and always picks up small rocks to add to her collection to remember fun places she has been. She lines them up on the windowsill in her kitchen in Burlington, Connecticut.